I0750265

FINISHING LINE PRESS
www.finishinglinepress.com

SIT WILD

poems by

Mo Fowler

Finishing Line Press
Georgetown, Kentucky

SIT WILD

ISBN 978-1-64662-595-6 First Edition

ACKNOWLEDGMENTS

This sweaty little chapbook is something I wrote a couple years ago now, and the process of getting from then to here would not have been possible without

Andrea, who read every iteration of these poems and, as always, made sense of me.
My family, for being a safe place to land, and a guaranteed laugh.
Sarah, for taking me in—in every sense of the word, and offering a friendship where I can be my all.
Those who are a home to me as much as any city has ever been: Darcy, Amber, Ava, and Nat
Everyone who gave me days to look forward to while I was working all the jobs these poems are about, but especially Nayelli.
The whole team at Finishing Line.

Publisher: Leah Huete de Maines
Editor: Christen Kincaid
Cover Art: Mo Fowler
Author Photo: Mo Fowler
Cover Design: Elizabeth Maines McCleavy

Order online: www.finishinglinepress.com
also available on amazon.com

Author inquiries and mail orders:
Finishing Line Press
PO Box 1626
Georgetown, Kentucky 40324
USA

Table of Contents

for every version of me I had to leave behind to survive

FOR ALL I KNOW

I am doing everything wrong—
should not live here, or should not
send texts with prayer hands as periods
or pick through the lukewarm sweet potato
cubes that lay orange going gray
in a Tupperware on my lunch break
or suck lemons in the morning
cut in half, in half
in half like fresh fruit
could make me feel my use
like here: I made a whole sunshine
of slices in my palm,
You're welcome,
should not slap my sandals against concrete
on the walk to the corner store in a rain
storm to buy more fruit that will wait
to save my life on the bedside table
or stack the largest book on top
in the pile on the windowsill or notice
how all twelve lipsticks, shelved in my medicine
cabinet stand shoulder
to shoulder arranged
by shade of purple, pink, orange,
red—maybe I am all wrong.
Maybe red comes first.

IN THE INTERVIEW

they ask how many pounds
I can deadlift.

They do not ask me to prove
it & interviews are sweaty

beds of "I'll be better" so in that room
I can deadlift one hundred and thirty pounds.

In that room I can completely erase
the weight of my own steps

on the earth. My feet in small black flats
I hide beneath the table.

They believe me enough to move on
to other questions, don't mention

that once I start the job the men
will try to lift everything for me—

My strength is a new mother—

I will find it in the falling
car of their conviction that I can't do anything,

cause I got this job and I still answer every question
like *I will be better,* and I will

be better and I will put my boots
on at five every morning and if I get somewhere

if I get—better—I better, I deadlift my self, up
over my head.

SOUR CUT

I am anything.
Today I am lemon scent-
ed Lysol. I am dripping
down the steps—a lost
cause, last shot,
glitchy timeclock
shows I'm always one
minute early.

I am anything.
Today I am pepper spray
in a leather sheaf snapped
shut. I am thrumming
with potential threat—a lost
heart, last call, butter-
colored mums with
a single ivory peony.

I am anything.
Today I am trying
hard. Harder. This life
is a hinting glimpse—
the corner of a slice
of lemon, eyes shut
at the tart slap, mouth wet
for more.

CAN I HELP YOU FIND ANYTHING TODAY?

They ask about the new eight
billion liter tankless water heaters
that we have down aisle six.

They ask if I have a boyfriend.
They ask where the 24-bit Drexel drills
with extensions are, they ask

why I work here,
they ask where can I find this screw? Sometimes
they wink when they say screw.

They ask can you find someone to help me?
They ask why the new Goodyear 50-foot
MAXLite rubber hose is infused with vanilla scent.

They ask, don't you people know that my wife
loves it when I lay my tinged-black rubber stink
rough hands on her cheeks and I smell like

hard work? Don't you know my wife needs me
to work hard, to smell like rubber, to come to stores
like this and not need to ask you

for anything? They ask me to pick out
a color in the Sherwin-Williams semi-gloss
that matches the hand-me-down couch from their brother

who they don't talk to much anymore but
this color, this color, this color could fix things, maybe, right?
They ask, don't I think they could have a family

again? They ask will the six-foot fiddleleaf fig or the shade-friendly peace
lily look better in the corner of the living room where my wife used to—

used to read.

They ask why I'm not smiling.
They ask me to smile more.
They ask if I'm sick, if I'm tired, if I'm okay

carrying that. They ask me to sit down with them a second,
see, I just had surgery and it was the scariest day
of my life, and now every day is scary too so I need to sit a minute.

They ask why I'm not in school. They ask why I even bothered going
to school. They always ask the guy standing next to me
first.

I ask, can I help you find anything today?
They say no.
They laugh.
They say, a hose that smells enough like rubber that women
will look me in the eye again.

PORTRAIT OF MYSELF AS POPEYE

They have been painting
the hallway outside my
apartment for hours.

Two of them and their soft
rock music on a radio that bumps
its head down the stairs

each time they finish a swath
of plaster. They laugh middle
school through my door

their brushes sound like feet
shuffled in thick carpet
and sometimes a dry scrape

racket of them in here with me.
I smell the paint in wafts,
flashes that match their falsetto-

disguised voices singing along
scratching up and down
up and down. At work I mix paint

colors for contractors who ask
if I'm sure I know how, and I do
know that one fleck of paint

hardener, inhaled, could kill
them in their bloodstream.
I ease gallons onto my shoulders

like I am so strong. I want
to write a poem about how I am
so strong, but outside my door they laugh

they gasp
            they crack, slap back.
I jump,

feel the thin of every layer
of drywall between the harsh
scrape of their brush

against me, and my hand
on the scarred 1944 wall of my apartment—
my own my own my own

I make fists behind the door, I make
muscles, hold my biceps up and growl silently.
They bump the wall again and my hand

tremors in its coil. Don't they know
I am trying to write a poem about how I
am so strong

THE DISHES HAVE TO SOAK FOREVER

I will be late for my shift because I am staring
at the dishes: an alabaster ceramic bowl
smeared violent carmine from the berries
in my morning oatmeal, nesting inside a frying
pan crusted from frozen
potstickers that popped a spastic spray—
oil, small burnt circles on my chest

now in the water, the pan hits
a sunshine diner mug from an estate
sale—it has rings from black coffee gone dry
inside of it like a tree, or tea leaves
telling the future & past that a tub
peanut butter, used up
soaks in the sludge so I can plant
catnip in the plastic jar later I will

wash them when I get home or
after dinner or when the email comes
saying I got the job or that might
be never so I will wash them when I
finish the laundry or when I work
less than six days a week or when someone
else threatens—promises—
to walk through my door.

ALL THE ANGRY WOMEN BOX, NOW

I am too broke
for boxing, I have no time
for angry—I scream in the car
between shifts, I am too busy
to take classes on threading
a needle of rage
through each of my knuckles
and into the hollow
vinyl sweat of the bag.

My anger gets lost on its way
out of me. I try to cough the trembling
cardinal mucus up my throat,
off my aching organs
out of me, but end up in bed
leg hair catching on flannel
sheets, while the guys
play basketball in the street hoop
below my window, the sound like

"Hey! Here Here Here
Here Here!"

I set five-minute alarms
to not-quite-nap, make myself eat
pesto, eat pita bread, put on pants.
Lift a foot, lift another, slip silken
into the make-believe required of me.
Make myself stay alive. Make myself
whatever it takes to get through.
Below the window
they shout

"Here! Here
Here Here Here
Here!"

and I am.

MOTHERING MY ROTTING SELF

I did everything anyone ever
asked so that I might walk to the kitchen
in dirty underwear on my day off
with hair nested, eyes a violet sag, to bake
a morning pie. That's all I wanted. To live
in a quiet place. No television
playing riddles up the back of my neck
at six am skittering the thin skin
of my inner arms. No one asking
what are you doing, or why? To live
in this apartment that holds no assumptions
a barely draining shower where I can dye
my hair, work dead-end jobs in silence. To live
with peanut butter in my cupboard,
honey on my oatmeal, and rent
I can mostly afford. I hold my breath
a mouth full of pearls—sometimes I gasp them
onto the unswept kitchen floor. Luminous
white shine in the fluorescence of my fridge.

I'm learning so many different ways to stare
the luck of my life in the face. Like baking
a rich chocolate pie with the sunrise
I'm learning that flour sifted across
my palms is the same constellation of dust
as white chalk stuck to the dry calluses
at seven, on the bars, and I always trusted
my hands to catch me. That I might trust
my hands again. That I might trust the thin skin
of my inner arms. I eat a single slice
of the pie and it is perfect—each minute
direction of the recipe realized. It is creamy
opulence with flaky crust and tastes
like decay on my tongue. I leave the rest
to mold over
all month.

HOUSESITTING IN THE SUBURBS

I have too many blood-tipped
mosquito bites to be spreading my bare toes
on the Persian carpets of this house. I itch
instead of listen as the cashmere woman
expounds on instructions for how to live
in her house while they're gone.

It is a house
where you just know—hovering
in the driveway—that there is a gleaming office
on the second floor with bookcases hand-
carved from redwoods her husband's great-great-grandfather
planted in a copse in the backyard, with beveled windows
he wipes down every Sunday and a mahogany ship
captain's desk where he shuffles
at six am in loafers and gray chinos
a quarter-zip sweater pushed up to his
elbows and a coffee brought in by
his wife, which he drinks
while talking stocks over speakerphone.

I take walks in the lavender mornings, wearing
his sweaters, the dog not pulling
on the leash. I rearrange
their silverware and then the board games
in a chestnut hutch on the living room's edges
where the wood sweats citrus cleaner. I rest my cheek
against it, leave an oil patch that smears
when I try to wipe it off.

I text the wife every single morning
for the wifi code, the messages sit on a growing string
of unread beads and I start to send
them just to add to the satisfying swath
of blue that fills the screen. It is a building
wave, and crests in anticlimactic
suds after two weeks, someone responds

You have the wrong number, please stop

I shoulder into the daughter's room
on the third floor in what would be a turret if
you were to admit this is more than a house.
I jump at the shock
of fur on the bed
thinking it is the dog somehow in this closed
room but it is stuffed. There is no cocaine or condoms
the dresser drawers are all socks and loose, used batteries.

While I sit at his desk after my walk
his caramel coffee warming my hand
through the mug I hope he always uses, I message
the husband instead the next morning. The dog
at my feet around my bare toes
its belly warm blood and bug bitten, I wonder
if he does this. I wonder if he rubs
bare dew damp toes on his dog's belly and pretends
to be himself
every morning.

MERCHANDISE MAINTENANCE

When people ask what I do
I never tell the truth—which is that
I manufacture living conditions.

At five am I show up to the warehouse
where the fluorescence leeches
the break room. I burp coffee, switch out
the night crew, all their earbuds
still in and I begin a day
that has already ended.

In the glow of the overhead track lighting
I rearrange the new snake plant shipment
so they grow towards a glass sun, check
the roots growing back in on themselves
against the walls of the pot for signs of rot
from sitting water.

On the toilet I scroll twitter, I wince
at where I am breaking out
along the sweaty lines of my apron,
I lean a fingertip into the metallic soil
of the plants in my section, angle a fan
to blow make believe wind
through their branches.

My manager calls me to the back
to watch this week's corporate training video
on how to take care of yourself
at work. I find a third of a bag of Lays
rolled to a tube in my apron pocket—it is close
enough to food to count as breakfast.

Moving my hips to the pumped-in music,
I fill the thick plastic jug to the marked line:
the predetermined level of water they need
to stay alive long enough
to sell.

TRADITION

"everyone wanting
to make their own kind of America,
but still be America, too."
—from "Roadside Attractions with the Dogs of
America" by Ada Limón

I.

It is a tradition of mornings

so early adrenaline plucks
a few optimistic notes
across my ribs as I pull on
a tired bra, jeans with mud
already dried into the seams

so early the breeze trills
eager fingers over my scalp
as I drive into the sun
smeared like yolk behind the glinting
skyline that scaffolds the freeway

so early even a burned sip
tastes good from the first
of my two morning coffees, when I clock
in one of the lifers on the butt dimpled couch
in the breakroom yawns toward me
Oh you brought one for me,
how sweet

so early that the plastic melt frosting
from the morning meeting donuts
to thank us for showing up again
drops a stain onto my apron
dabbing at it in the bathroom

sink, I make mirror eye contact
with a customer who recognizes
me from somewhere. It is a tradition of being known
by my dream and by every other person
chasing after it.

II.

It is the American Dream to drive

from one job to the next
while I eat cold black beans and bagged salad
balanced across my thighs as I try to see the street
signs this late at night, I clock in as the radio
station shifts to a smooth talk advice show,
wrangle through the throat bite of the Monster
the manager buys me for facing the aisles
so fast, each sip dissolving
my saliva in its tracks

to drive home at one am
listening to a podcast about the job
market while I slide damp
goldfish crackers from a baggie
that's been sunbathing on the passenger seat
for weeks, into my cheeks and let their
orange hyper bodies soften,
soften, swallow

to drive twice the speed limit
through thin, congested streets
while I insist over speakerphone
to my parents, two time zones away,
in the furthest thing from my customer
service voice, that I'm doing

alright, *No I am, no I promise*
this is what I want
this is on the way to what I want
I could come—I could come to want this

to drive fast enough
that I am confident
the momentum of my life
is forward

III.

It is time-honored

that the adrenaline clogs somewhere in the bottom
of the first coffee—in time for my eight minute nap
in the Shar Pei folds of Lysol-sprayed faux leather
of that breakroom couch

that I drag the sun-yellow mop bucket
into the men's room and find that someone has again
wiped their own shit on the wall

that I eat vending machine Doritos
for two different meals in
one day—I am part of history
this history of trying
and trying and trying
to be good enough to scrape a fleck
from the ceiling of this country
that when I get a third job I am steel-
spined knowing that I will be fine
because it is tradition

It is American

I will work
three jobs and barely make
rent and I will feel proud. I mean
shame. I mean proud. I mean—

WHEN I WAKE UP I AM NOTHING AT ALL

that I would recognize. I am dredging
on locked thumbs toward the miracle
corner of the kitchen's gone-gray linoleum
where my four dollar coffee pot sits
in a continent of stains I never
clean up. I see characters
in the loose shapes
of the mess, shake my head
to clear them, spill
hot flow over the lips
of my daisy yellow mug,
coffee steaming dark
onto the bleeding seams of my knuckles
cracked open in the dry January air
in a quiet moment between the cars
that drive past this shaking
room—the morning is vast
in every direction
still, there is no way to get
what I want in this life
but every sunrise
is beasting and battles
and I would rather be bloody
than nothing at all.

NOT EVERYONE GETS OUT, BUT WE ALL GET GLIMPSES

I get the call
at the end of my shift
staring at an apple
browning in the cup holder,
my car seat greasy beneath
me from sunscreen smeared thighs,
and in that third floor parking garage
I have won
the fight.
I know
that I will live
I stay silent
I sit wild

Mo Fowler is a queer writer with previous work in *Zone 3* and *Motley Mag*, currently pursuing MFA candidacy at UC Irvine and would love to hear from you at mocfowler@gmail.com

www.ingramcontent.com/pod-product-compliance
Lightning Source LLC
LaVergne TN
LVHW051023080826
845145LV00009B/2777

* 9 7 8 1 6 4 6 6 2 5 9 5 6 *